Marilyn

Nick Yapp

FALL RIVER PRESS

contents

1

BORN AND BRED
IN DIFFICULT TIMES

In the summer of 1926, Hollywood was proceeding on its merry, profitable, and silent way – hit films of the year included *What Price Glory?*, starring Victor McLaglen and Dolores del Rio, and Cecil B. DeMille's *The Volga Boatman*, in which Elinor Fair played the part of the lovely Princess Vera. Two shattering milestones of the cinema lay ahead. The first, only three years away, was the coming of the Talkies. The second, happening then and there, was the coming of Marilyn Monroe.

She was born to Gladys Baker, *née* Monroe (*right*), and either a Norwegian immigrant named Edward Mortenson, or Stanley Gifford, a co-worker with Gladys at RKO studios in Los Angeles. Doubt and confusion surrounded little Norma Jeane Baker from the very beginning. Monroe herself certainly wished and frequently fantasized that her real father was Clark Gable. Like all her homespun fairy tales, it turned out to be untrue.

Monroe arrived in the world on the Glorious First of June, 1926. From the start, Fate did not smile on Norma Jeane (*above at six months*). There were already signs of serious emotional disturbance in her mother, who hurriedly left her baby to the day-care of others, and returned to her job as a film cutter.

A SHAKY START

Later in life, Monroe was to tell many tales about her early life. There was the Gable fixation; the attempt by her maternal grandmother, Delia Monroe, to smother little Norma Jeane when she was only thirteen months old; the frequent changes of foster parents; and the long history of being abused and molested. All the time, in the background, was the lurking menace of insanity in the family. Delia Monroe was sent to a mental hospital where she died at the age of fifty-one, and Gladys Baker suffered from recurrent bouts of schizophrenia. Some of the stories were true, others weren't. Over the years, Monroe came to believe all of them.

Photographs of Monroe as a toddler rarely reveal any early hints of the twinkling eyes and flashing smile that were to emblazon the covers of so many magazines twenty years later. Norma Jeane was chubby, with an almost permanent frown on her face. She was a worrier, and her worries were to multiply and intensify as she grew older. While America publicly danced and secretly drank its way towards the Wall Street Crash, Monroe was learning that life was hard, bruising, and threatening.

Above: Gladys Baker (*second from left*) with her baby Norma Jeane (*third from left*) and friends on a Californian beach in 1929.

Above: A studio portrait of toddler Norma Jeane Baker, probably commissioned by her maternal grandmother, Delia Monroe.

Opposite: A rare happy picture of Norma Jeane from 1929 when she was three.

"*I learned to walk as a baby and I haven't had a lesson since.*"

From the beginning, baby Norma Jeane's entire family edifice was founded on delusion, misrepresentation and outright lies. Her mother's mind flitted so often between reality and fantasy that she may well have ultimately convinced herself that Norma Jeane's older siblings – Jackie and Bernice – were dead. The truth was that they had been taken by their father when Gladys Baker's marriage broke up. Norma Jeane did not hear about her brother and sister until she was twelve years old, by which time Bernice was fifteen and Jackie was dead. He had died three years earlier, in 1935, following an illness that his father would not allow doctors to treat.

Norma Jeane was born of parents who were both dangerously dysfunctional.

Left: Norma Jeane at age four, with another friend.
Opposite: Norma Jeane (*on right*) in 1930.

THE ORPHAN

As the United States slumped into economic depression, Norma Jeane tottered through her early childhood. To those around her, she was the illegitimate single child of a one-parent family, and in the late Twenties and early Thirties this was not a propitious start in life for any child. Her mother was not a cruel woman, but neither was she a good mother. There were many times when she wasn't a mother at all. Mental instability lay at the heart of her treatment of Norma Jeane. And never

seeing her real father, never even certain of who he was, paved the way for fantasies that lasted Monroe's entire life.

For little Norma Jeane, emotionally crippling infancy was followed by years of being moved from one adult to another, from one institution to another, with little or no continuity, affection, or reassurance in these formative years. "Home" didn't exist. In her mid-thirties, Monroe became a patient of Dr. Ralph Greenson, a well-established Californian psychiatrist. He immediately recognised that Monroe

presented herself in therapy as an anxious child: "…like an orphan, a waif, and she masochistically provokes people to mistreat her and take advantage of her." The problem was that, appalling as her childhood had been, Monroe's imagination created an even worse scenario of her own past. What remained, for the rest of her life, was an insatiable longing for love and sympathy.

THE TRAUMA TRAIL

One episode from her childhood that Monroe "remembered" many times throughout her life, reportedly took place when she was eight years old. She was then living with foster parents who took in lodgers, one of whom was a man named Kimmel. Monroe alleged that Kimmel had enticed her into his room and had assaulted her. She ran to her foster mother, who told her to keep her mouth shut. Kimmel was a "good" lodger who paid his rent promptly.

At the age of nine, Norma Jeane was sent to a private orphanage in Hollywood, where she lived with sixty other children. She remained a loner, however, and recalled, as an adult, how she "used to sit in the window and cry because I could see RKO and I knew that my mother worked there..."

Then came school days at Emerson Junior High, Westwood where the gangling young student was nicknamed Norma Jean String Bean. Her science teacher, Mabel Ella Campbell, remembered her as "a little girl, not well developed... a nice child, not very outgoing, not very vibrant..."

Above: The little girl enters adolescence: Norma Jeane, aged twelve, poses for the camera with one of her foster parents, Ana Lower, seated behind. Ana was the aunt of her guardian, Grace McKee.

Opposite: The classic Monroe looks begin to emerge – Norma Jeane Baker at fourteen.

Norma Jeane (*center*) with friends in 1941. Monroe later claimed that it was about this time that she had a baby, and that the baby was taken away from her by Grace McKee, her guardian, and given up for adoption.

THE LOST CHILD

The adult Monroe lost count of the number of abortions and miscarriages that occurred in her life. There is no doubt that she longed to have a baby, and Monroe repeatedly claimed to have given birth to a baby boy when she was fourteen or fifteen years old. She also claimed that the baby was taken from her by the authorities at the insistence of the woman who was at that time her guardian.

"I hugged and kissed him... I just kept touching him. I couldn't believe he was my baby... But the doctor and a nurse came in with Grace (her guardian)... They took my baby from me... and I never saw him again..." Monroe had another version of the same incident, in which she opted to give the baby up for adoption, and was then overwhelmed with the fear that God would punish her.

Whatever the truth was, it was yet another sign that Monroe's hold on reality was already tenuous and intermittent.

The first marriage…
Opposite: Norma Jeane and James Dougherty at Avalon, Santa Catalina Island during Dougherty's basic training in the wartime Merchant Marine.
Above: Dougherty, Norma Jeane (*on left*), and friend in 1943.

THE FIRST MARRIAGE

It was Grace McKee who arranged Monroe's first marriage. Grace had recently married and planned to move East without taking Norma Jeane with her. It was not the first, nor the last time that Monroe was to be passed from one home to another, one carer to another, and ultimately one man to another. Grace looked about her and decided that Jim Dougherty would be the man to relieve her of her teenage ward.

Dougherty was an athletic young man who liked young women in general and Norma Jeane in particular. He liked the way she danced – close and intimate – and the fact that she laughed a lot and knew when to keep her mouth shut. This last talent was to be challenged to breaking point as Monroe staggered through the last desperate years of her life.

Norma Jeane and Dougherty were married on June 19, 1942, three weeks after her sixteenth birthday. Two days later, Jim went back to his work as a night-fitter at Lockheed Aviation.

"I don't want to make money.
I just want to be wonderful.."

Opposite: No longer Norma Jeane Baker, but now
Marilyn Monroe, the twenty-one-year-old Hollywood
hopeful poses for the camera in 1947.

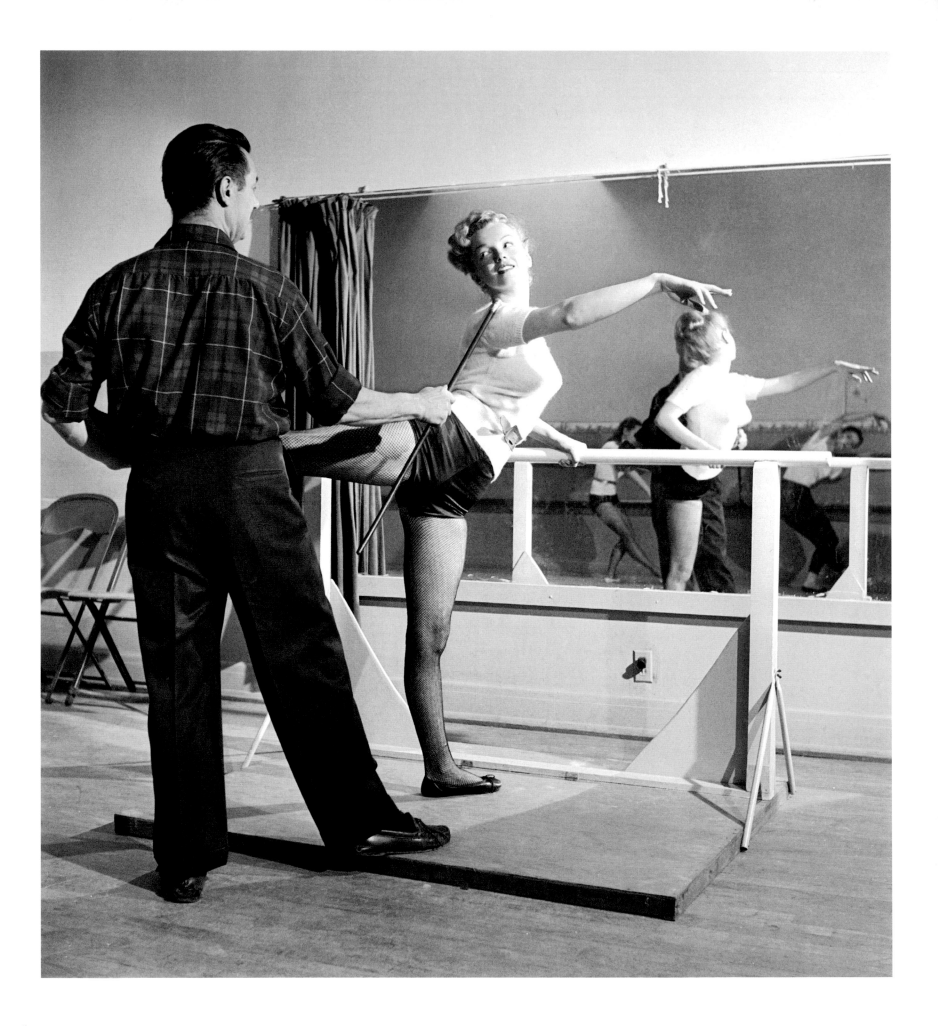

BECOMING MARILYN

While husband Jim Dougherty was serving overseas, Norma Jeane worked for Radio Plane, a small factory that made aircraft for target practice. Here she was visited by an army photographer named David Conover. Conover's mission was to take "morale-boosting shots" of pretty girls for *Yank* magazine. Struck by the beauty of her eyes and the contents of her red sweater, Conover persuaded Norma Jeane that she had all it took to become a cover-girl.

It may have been the deciding factor in the break-up of her first marriage. Dougherty told her she would have to choose between modelling and marriage. He heard of her decision while in China, via a lawyer's letter. Norma Jeane had filed for divorce.

Conover's pictures got Norma Jeane on the books of the Blue Book Model Agency, and she was soon featured in a number of girlie magazines. The following year, she posed for, and had a brief affair with, another photographer, Andre de Dienes. One thing led to another, and in 1946 she was given a contract as a stock player with Twentieth Century-Fox. The name on the contract was "Marilyn Monroe".

Opposite: Marilyn Monroe at a Hollywood dance class, February 1947. She was an enthusiastic student of ballet (see over).
Above: The young Monroe back on the beach in 1948.

"Looking back, I guess I used
to play-act all the time.
For one thing, it meant I could
live in a more interesting world
than the one around me."

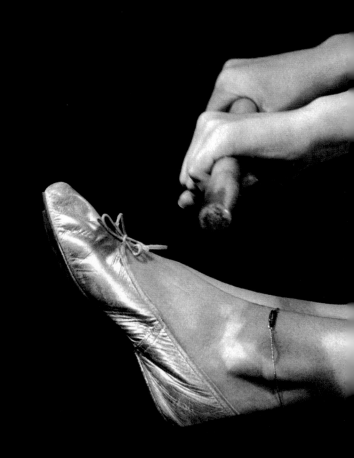

Right: A publicity photo of the young Marilyn Monroe, as a trapeze artist (1948).
Left: In her first Hollywood credited movie, Monroe, as Peggy Martin, (*front, second from right*) flashes her smile in Phil Karlson's *Ladies of the Chorus*.

A START IN HOLLYWOOD – LADIES OF THE CHORUS

There was never a shortage of old men, young men, and middle-aged men taking an interest in Monroe. From the moment she entered Tinseltown, a queue of would-be sponsors and lovers rapidly formed, eager to praise and adore, to handle and exploit her.

Like many others, Robert Slatzer, a nineteen-year-old journalist, thought there was something different about her. Ben Lyon (forty-five, and an ex-movie star) thought "she had a good face". Bill Burnside (forty-three, and the J. Arthur Rank Organisation's Hollywood representative) believed "she had it there, all right, that star quality..." James Bacon (a veteran Hollywood columnist) was more outspoken: "My God! There was something about this girl. The moment you met her you knew she was going to make it..."

In March 1948, Monroe was loaned on a six-month, $75 a week contract to Columbia Pictures, where studio boss Harry Cohn licked his lips and looked to the future.

Gaining in confidence, but always with that self-doubt about her glamorous appeal.
Above: A studio portrait of Marilyn Monroe, in 1947.
Opposite: A photograph on location at a swimming pool in 1948.

LOVE HAPPY?

In the spring of 1949, Artists' Alliance were looking for a young woman with a sexy walk for a small part in the last Marx Brothers film. By trimming a quarter of an inch from the heel of one shoe, Monroe had developed a walk that turned most male heads. She paraded for Groucho Marx, who saw her as "Theda Bara, Mae West and Bo-Peep all rolled into one." The part was hers.

The film was called *Love Happy*, a condition that Monroe never experienced in real life. The part was tiny, but David Miller, the director, saw the talents that Monroe could bring to the film's publicity campaign. Monroe was sent to New York, where she posed for *Photoplay* magazine, renewed her private and professional relationship with Andre de Dienes, visited El Morocco – New York's top nite-spot – and met millionaire dress manufacturer Henry Rosenfeld.

Over the remaining thirteen years of her life, Monroe was frequently to confide in Rosenfeld, a man who kept his love for her under strict control, but let his affection for her flourish. There seems little doubt that he genuinely cared for her, soaking up as much as he could of her outpourings of woe and anxiety, lending her money, keeping her secrets, and paying her often considerable legal fees. He did all that a real father might have done, but even this was too little, too late as far as Monroe was concerned.

ENTERING THE JUNGLE

Though her part in *Love Happy* was simply a cameo role, it raised Monroe's profile in Hollywood. Her next movie was a far more serious affair. She played the part of Angela Phinlay, a gangster's mistress, in John Huston's *The Asphalt Jungle*, a part that enabled her to display true acting ability and led to a seven-year contract at $500 a week with Fox. Huston had no doubt about her talent: "She went right down into her personal experience for everything... She had no techniques. It was all the truth, it was only Marilyn..."

Marilyn began to move in Hollywood's higher circles. She met Billy Wilder, Nunally Johnson, Sam Spiegel, and Spyros Skouras, the President of Twentieth Century-Fox. Professionally her star was rising. Privately, she remained low. She lost a key father figure in her life, her agent and lover Johnny Hyde. Hyde died in December 1950. A few days after his funeral, Monroe made her third serious suicide attempt.

Opposite: "Mirror, mirror on the wall..." A picture of Monroe while on tour at Warrenburg, New York in 1949.
Above: A studio portrait taken in the same year. It was about this time, penniless and without work, that Monroe posed naked for the famous calendar of photographer Tom Kelley.

Monroe on tour, promoting *Love Happy...*
Left: Monroe with fellow film actor Don Defore –
who always played the "regular guy", "the good ole
boy from next door" – on board a train from Los
Angeles to New York.
Right: At the WWSC radio studios in New York City.

DETERMINED TO SUCCEED

Monroe was in her mid-twenties, already a minor celebrity, known for the daring clothes she wore to formal Hollywood celebrations, the famous walk that she could turn on and off like a tap, and for the power to inject pure seduction into her voice when the occasion demanded it.

What the woman, who had just become *Miss Cheesecake* to GIs fighting the Korean War, really wanted, however, was to be taken seriously as an actress. She already had one acting coach at Fox, now she took a second – Michael Chekhov, an ex-pupil of the great Stanislavsky. Chekhov introduced her to the classics, from Shakespeare to the works of his own uncle. Monroe was

grateful. She told Chekhov: "I want to be an artist, not an erotic freak. I don't want to be sold to the public as a celluloid aphrodisiac..."

She began a process of self-education, reading Proust and Rilke, listening to classical music, studying the works of great painters, seeking out intellectuals. She believed her own childhood had suffered as much from lack of cerebral stimulation as from lack of emotional nourishment. Living alone, in a tiny apartment, she did all she could to make up for lost time.

It was at this stage in her life, when she was ravenously hungry for culture, that she first met Arthur Miller.

"Hollywood
is a place where they'll
pay you a thousand dollars
for a kiss and fifty cents
for your soul."

2
CHAPTER TWO

HEADING FOR THE STARS

In June 1950, Monroe celebrated her twenty-fourth birthday. It was not a happy birthday - her 1948 Ford convertible had recently been repossessed. She was then living in North Palm Drive, Beverly Hills. It was her twentieth place of residence, and there were twenty-seven more to come. She had sacrificed body, if not soul, to make it in Hollywood, where an orthodontist had fixed her teeth and a surgeon had "perfected" her nose and chin. So far she had made seven films, in two of which she had been un-credited, and even her most devoted fans were happy to forget them all. Nearly sixty years after the filming of *Love Happy*, most people remember Monroe's performance only for Groucho's on-screen reaction to her - a two-minute revival of old vaudeville.

A publicity still from 1950 (*above*). Monroe with James Brown and Mickey Rooney in a still from Tay Garnett's *The Fireball*, a tale of juvenile delinquency and roller-skating (*right*).

INTO THE JUNGLE

John Huston's *The Asphalt Jungle*
provided Monroe with the breakthrough
she'd been looking for. The part of
Angela Phinley - mistress of Louis
Calhern's sardonic and crooked
millionaire lawyer - was a good one. The
film had a great script and was praised
by critics and moviegoers alike, though
Louis B. Mayer, head of MGM (who
made the film) hated it. "That Asphalt
Pavement thing is full of nasty, ugly
people doing nasty things," he said. "I
wouldn't walk across the room to see a
thing like that."

Huston won an Academy Award
nomination as director of *The Asphalt*
Jungle, and he reckoned the film saved
Monroe's career. "Marilyn was one step
from oblivion when I directed her... She
impressed me more off the screen than
on. There was something touching and
appealing about her." The success of the
film led to Twentieth Century-Fox
casting Marilyn for the part of Claudia
Casswell in Joseph L. Mankiewicz's *All*
About Eve, another highly-rated and
commercially successful film. Monroe
was now working with some of the
cream of Hollywood players – many of
them women (Jean Hagen in *The Asphalt*
Jungle; Bette Davis, Celeste Holm, Anne
Baxter and Thelma Ritter in *All About*
Eve). She was among real actors, and
she applied herself diligently to learning
their craft. She had spent three days
with her coach, Natasha Lytess, going
through the script of *Jungle* before
auditioning for the part.

The immediate aftermath of *All About*
Eve was disappointing. Monroe appeared
in three deeply mediocre comedies –
Love Nest, Let's Make It Legal, and
Hometown Story – as well as the part of
a streetwalker in a compilation film of
five O. Henry short stories (*O. Henry's*
Full House). Monroe was not yet in orbit,
but she had achieved lift-off.

REFINING THE IMAGE

During working hours, Monroe was seldom far away from a camera. The studio publicity departments loved to pose and parade her, with or without just cause. It wasn't that it was impossible to take a bad picture of Monroe, it was that any and every photographic session was bound to yield one or two shots of breath-taking excellence. Lee Strasberg, founder of the Actor's Studio, and one of Monroe's many acting coaches from the mid-1950s onwards, noted that Monroe's "quality when photographed is almost of a supernatural beauty". Billy Wilder, who directed her in two films, remarked: "She had flesh which photographed like flesh. You feel you can reach out and touch it.'" Many photographers who worked with beautiful women every day, saw something so special about Monroe's beauty that they fell in love with her – some secretly, several openly. The first photographer she ever worked with, David Conover, described her as "a photographer's dream".

Left: The 1950 search for the right pose, the right costume, the right hair style continues.
Opposite: 1951 – a home shot, but whose home and why and on what occasion is unknown. The bikini is modest by later standards, but 1951 was the year the bikini was banned from the *Miss World* competition.

THE CELLULOID JUNGLE

Professionally, 1952 opened for Monroe with the role of platinum blonde Lois Laurel in Howard Hawks's *Monkey Business*. The film was produced by another of Monroe's growing body of admirers, Sol Siegel. Cary Grant and Ginger Rogers did what they could with the story of a chimpanzee that discovers the elixir of youth, but the film was not a success. Monroe came out of it well, however. The public liked the new presentation of her as a beacon of slinky allure, and she made the cover of *Life* magazine on April 7 that year. There was no feature article about her, that spot was held by a long piece about flying saucers.

Monroe was now a celebrity, albeit a second league one. Newspapers covered her illnesses, which occurred with worrying frequency, and set out to report or fabricate tales of likely romances. When baseball star and national hero Joe DiMaggio visited the set of *Monkey Business*, the two were immediately linked romantically. Outwardly, Monroe appeared to be happy with all of this; inwardly, it fed the neuroses that were to plague her all her life.

Above: With her back to the wall, Monroe faces the ladies and gentlemen of the Press, 1951.
Opposite: Monroe at a dinner to mark the world premiere of *Cinerama*, at the Cocoanut Grove, Los Angeles, September 30, 1952. With her are the columnist Loella Parsons and Jack Martin, the club's *maitre d'hotel*.

50 *Marilyn*

The 1951 photographic quest continues...
Right: Monroe in a swimsuit to warn of
the danger from July Fourth fireworks —
what will those PR guys think of next?
Left: Almost there... the sultry look begins
to burn through.

Two shots from September 1951 showing Monroe in the office of Jerry Wald, who produced *Clash by Night*.
Left: Wald and Monroe - the producer examines the product.
Far left: Monroe reads through the film's screenplay. Wald was a fan of Monroe, not for her serious acting, but because he considered her "the greatest *farceuse* in the business, a female Chaplin".

CLASH BY NIGHT AND DAY

Despite being cast in increasingly bigger roles in increasingly prestigious movies, Monroe was still widely regarded as a pin-up girl, perhaps the best there has ever been. In 1951 alone, she was voted "The present all GIs would like to find in their Christmas stocking"; "The Girl Most Likely to Thaw Alaska" (by GIs in the Aleutian Islands; "The Girl Most Wanted to Examine" (by the 7th Division Medical Corps); and "The Girl They Would Like to Intercept" (by members of the All Weather Fighter Squadron).

What such lascivious attention did to Monroe time would later show. For the moment, she seemed to accept and enjoy it. Undoubtedly, there was much of the exhibitionist in her, accompanied by a ready wit. On one occasion, feigning innocence, she asked an audience of some 10,000 US marines: "I don't know why you boys are always getting so excited about sweater girls. Take away their sweaters and what have they got?" It may not have been her own line, but the spot-on delivery was all hers.

Left and opposite: Monroe in the button-front dress that she wore to the Hollywood Entertainers Baseball Game (accompanied by Mickey Rooney) in Los Angeles during the summer of 1952. It was a style that she favored at the time, similar to a dress she wore the same year in *Clash by Night*.

ON
HER
KNEES

Back at Twentieth Century-Fox, after her brief spell with MGM, Monroe was once more in the hands of Darryl F. Zanuck, the head of the studio. There was a problem, though it is difficult today to know for sure precisely what it was. A young journalist named Robert Slatzer had been dating Monroe and wanted to marry her. Long after Monroe's death, there was talk of a wedding in Tijuana which, allegedly, took place on October 4, 1952.

According to Anthony Summers, whose book *Goddess* is one of the best accounts of Monroe's life, if the wedding did take place, the marriage lasted three days. The moment Monroe arrived back in Hollywood, Zanuck ordered that the marriage be brought to an immediate end. Within a week Monroe and Slatzer were back in Tijuana making sure that all evidence of the marriage was destroyed. Zanuck got what he wanted, protection of his investment. Monroe got what she wanted, her first leading role, playing the part of a deranged baby-sitter in *Don't Bother to Knock*.

Above: Monroe sits to apply make-up. The book beside her is *The Thinking Body* by Mabel Todd. It was a guide to ideokinesis, a way of using inner feeling and imagination to retrain the body to move with ease and balance.
Opposite: Monroe with fan mail received after the release of *The Asphalt Jungle*.

PROBLEMS OF MIND AND BODY

Consciously or subconsciously, Monroe spent much of her professional life building a dossier of bewildering misinformation about herself. She insisted to friends and other movie hopefuls that she had indeed married Slatzer, though no evidence of this has ever been found.

And, as well as misrepresenting her present, Monroe was constantly rewriting her past. In the summer of 1952, she told a magazine writer named Jim Henaghan that her mother had died when she was a child. Reporters soon established that Gladys Baker was alive, and was living in a mental asylum not far from Monroe's own Beverly Hills apartment. The story of Monroe's deceit or delusion was splashed across front pages. It did her career no harm.

Paranoia and hysteria were never far away. When she was admitted to hospital for the removal of her appendix in April 1952, she sent a note to the surgeon who was to operate, begging him to take extra care of her. It was the sort of letter that a highly literate toddler would have written if it could hold a pen in its tiny fist.

*"No one ever told me I was pretty
when I was a little girl.
All little girls should be told
they're pretty, even if they aren't.."*

As the search continued to find the "Monroe look", some photographers made the mistake of basing their portraits on re-runs of shots of former Hollywood stars – Swanson, Harlow, Dietrich, Grable et al.
Left: The ultimate in cheesecake… Monroe "projects" with animal intensity.
Right: More demure, but just as alluring. There were Monroe images to suit the taste of all male predators.

"It's not true that I had nothing on

I had the radio on."

THE NUDE CALENDAR

For all her difficulties in sorting reality from fantasy, Monroe had a well-organized business head when it came to self-promotion. Fox's publicity director, Harry Brand, acknowledged this when he described Monroe as "grooming herself to be the sexiest thing in pictures since Jean Harlow".

Monroe's ability to manipulate the media was never better displayed than when it emerged that she had once posed naked for a collection of calendar pictures taken by photographer Tom Kelley. Monroe's first response was to explain that they were taken three years earlier, on May 27, 1949, at a time when she had no film work, no modelling jobs, and virtually no money – she was paid only $50 for the session. The studio was mollified. Monroe then arranged to be interviewed by Aline Mosby, a female reporter with United Press International.

The interview was sympathetic. Monroe's reputation was saved. The studio was delighted. A year later, Hugh Hefner bought one of the nude pictures for $500 and made it the centerfold of the first edition of *Playboy*.

THE ICON APPEARS

Eisenstaedt was not the first *Life* photographer to take pictures of Monroe. Ed Clark, working for the same magazine, received a call from Fox early in Monroe's career, saying they had just signed a "hot tomato". Clark arranged sessions with Monroe. They went out to Griffith Park, and while Clark fired off rolls of film, Monroe sat and read poetry. Clark later recalled how he sent several rolls to *Life* in New York, but the magazine wired back, "Who the hell is Marilyn Monroe?" Clark was just a little ahead of time.

The camera always loved her, and so did most photographers, many of whom fell in love with her, some of whom became her lovers. The portraits of Monroe that have best withstood the test of time, however, are those taken by one of *Life's* founder photographers, Alfred Eisenstaedt. His approach was informal, seeking to make Monroe relaxed. The costume was perfect – rich black and white, with nothing to take the attention from Monroe's face. The lips were full, the eyes were heavy, the eyebrows accentuated almost to the point of taking flight. In Eisenstaedt's own word, "unbelievable".

Two studies from Eisenstaedt's 1953 photographic session with Monroe. A number of pictures failed to survive when Eisenstaedt made a rare miscalculation in the exposure he gave the color film on a number of rolls.

Left to right: Monroe in a still from
How to Marry a Millionaire; at the
Photoplay Gold Medal Awards dinner in
1953, at which she received the Award
for Most Popular Female Star; outside
Grauman's Chinese Theater; and in a
scene from *Gentlemen Prefer Blondes*.

THE DIMAGGIO AFFAIR

Monroe made three movies in 1953. In the first, *Niagara*, she played the part of Rose Loomis, a mentally unstable wife who is plotting to murder her husband. It was a big part in a big production, and Monroe received good reviews. The problem was that the studio couldn't resist exploiting "the walk", thereby devaluing the tension inherent in the film. It is perhaps the longest walk-away-from-camera shot in cinematic history, well worth it for Monroe fans, but unfair to Monroe's increasing desire to be taken seriously as an actor.

Her next film was a musical, *Gentlemen Prefer Blondes*, in which Monroe co-starred with an old high school acquaintance – Jane Russell. The two got on well. They had something in common: Russell was married to one ex-sports star; Monroe was seeking to marry another. If Monroe were to marry Joe DiMaggio, Russell advised that she should make sure she developed an intellectual and artistic life of her own. Monroe took note.

She had been courting DiMaggio for some time. When the Fox team left Los Angeles and headed east to shoot locations scenes for *Niagara*, Monroe spent time in New York, pursuing the man she believed she loved. It was the first anniversary of Jolting Joe's retirement from the game following a series of injuries. He was not a happy man. But Monroe's hopes of love rose anew when he made a surprise trip to be with her for Christmas 1952.

Left: Monroe with Humphrey Bogart and Lauren Bacall at the premiere of *How to Marry a Millionaire,* November 4, 1953.
Right: At the home of director Jean Negulesco on the night of the film's premiere.

HOW TO MARRY A MILLIONAIRE

Monroe was now making more than $1,000 a week. It wasn't a fortune, but she would never be out of work again. But there was a clash between Twentieth Century-Fox's plans for her, and Monroe's own professional ambitions. When Monroe was cast, with Betty Grable and Lauren Bacall, as one of the three young women looking for wealthy mates in *How to Marry a Millionaire*, she tried to debate her motivation in the role with director Jean Negulesco. He failed to appreciate that it was a serious question.

Nevertheless, both Negulesco and the film's producer Nunnally Johnson saw that Monroe was special, even by Hollywood standards. "She represents to man," said Negulesco, "something we all want in our unfulfilled dreams. A man, he's got to be dead not to be excited by her." To Johnson, Monroe was "a phenomenon of nature, like Niagara Falls and the Grand Canyon. All you can do is stand back and be awed by it."

15 August, 1953

PICTURE POST

MARILYN MONROE
AND JANE RUSSELL
IN
'GENTLEMEN
PREFER
BLONDES'
see inside

His Likes and Dislikes

LIFE

MARILYN MONROE
AND JANE RUSSELL
IN
'GENTLEMEN PREFER BLONDES'

20 CENTS

MAY 25, 1953

REG. U. S. PAT. OFF.

Cover Girl on both sides of
the Atlantic...
Far left: Jane Russell, Charles
Coburn, and Monroe pose
for a publicity still for
Gentlemen Prefer Blondes on
the cover of *Picture Post*,
August 15, 1953.
Left: Russell and Monroe, in
gowns designed by Billy
Travilla, on the cover of *Life*,
May 25, 1953.

GENTLEMEN PREFER BLONDES

Monroe was now unquestionably a celebrity, given star billing on every film. Studio staff addressed her as "Miss Monroe". But there were as ever problems. She had become increasingly dependent on pills. To get through each day she fed on a random mixture of "uppers" and "downers", and to get through each night she needed a cocktail of sleeping pills. Wherever she went, she took a plastic bag that rattled with its potent little pellets. Studio doctors prescribed them for her, and there were other medical practitioners ready to provide a back-up supply.

Despite the barbiturates and amphetamines, life on set was fun during the shooting of *Gentlemen Prefer Blondes*. Jane Russell was top star in the film, but Monroe took comfort from the fact that she, not Russell, was the Blonde. She enjoyed singing and dancing her way through the movie's two hit numbers – *Little Rock* and *Diamonds are a Girl's Best Friend* – giving the latter a solo performance that has come to be judged "iconic". She obtained her best reviews to date.

The film gained Monroe the distinction of being selected to add her handprints to the impressions of other Hollywood stars on the pavement outside Grauman's Chinese Theater (*above*, June 26, 1953). Monroe was sharp enough to know that neither she nor Russell had achieved fame through their hands. So, as they knelt down, Monroe suggested to Russell that the brunette should press her bosom into the wet cement, while the blonde sat in it – thus commemorating their major cinematic assets.

PROFESSIONAL TRIUMPHS, PRIVATE DISASTERS

By the mid-1950s, Monroe could do nothing wrong in front of a still camera. She knew how to use her face, body, eyes, and mouth, to deliver innocence, experience (*right*), the "come hither" look, pure happiness (*above*), what in older times would have labelled "slatternliness", and the wistfulness of the girl next door. In front of the movie cameras at Twentieth Century-Fox, however, there were times when she lost confidence, when her mouth dried up, but her eyes filled with tears. Monroe's hold on stability was becoming increasingly precarious. On the set of *Gentlemen Prefer Blondes*, Monroe collapsed after fellow actor Tommy Noonan likened her stage kiss to "being sucked by a vacuum". It was an unnecessarily cruel remark that a more hardened Hollywood goddess would have capped, but Monroe was always too vulnerable to hit back. She needed constant support and reassurance from all around her — make-up artists, co-stars, publicity agents, acting coaches, hairdressers, even dress designers.

"I'm very definitely a woman and I enjoy it.."

Sophistication replaces the raw sex appeal of the Nude Calendar. A horizontal Monroe poses for a well-dressed portrait in 1953.

Her fragility and indecision permeated her private life. She was insatiable in her demands for admiration, in her hunger to arouse sexual desire in many of the men she met. Monroe had developed a habit of apparently disorganized dating. She would often arrange for more than one male escort to arrive at roughly the same time on the same evening. Two beaux would stand awkwardly at Monroe's door, bouquets in hand, waiting to see which of them was to be honored with her company. Once she had decided, and that could take a while, the loser was charmingly, but swiftly, dismissed.

Billy Travilla, who worked as Monroe's dress designer on eight movies, and was briefly her lover, described her as an extremely bright woman, but with the whims of a child. She sent him a copy of the famous Nude Calendar, inscribed "Billy Dear, Please Dress Me Forever. I love you, Marilyn". Long after Monroe's death, Travilla told Anthony Summers, "I think she wanted to love, but could only love herself."

Left to right: Four head shots of Monroe, all dating from 1953. The beauty spot — enhanced in the Eisenstadt portraits — is masked here. It was the product of what has become known as "Monroe piercing".

UPS AND DOWNS

In the summer of 1953, Monroe moved into a new apartment on North Doheny Drive, Beverly Hills. She had a new car, a black Cadillac convertible, and new recognition. At the Golden Globe Awards, she was hailed as World Film Favorite, and *Harvard Lampoon* voted both *Gentlemen Prefer Blondes* and *How to Marry a Millionaire* among the Worst Films of the Year.

She was also about to have a new husband, though the romance between Monroe and DiMaggio was an affair that waxed hot and cold and was shot through with bitterness and

recrimination. He refused to accompany her to awards ceremonies, on the grounds that she dressed and conducted herself improperly — Billy Travilla had sewn her into her dress for the *Photoplay* Awards. DiMaggio spent much time spying on her, which was not unreasonable, given the way she behaved. When Monroe was filming in the Canadian Rockies, late in 1953, there were press reports that she had injured her leg. DiMaggio came running.

Monroe's problem was that she felt an almost permanent need to flaunt her sexuality, to practise her staggering ability

to arouse men, even those she met only briefly. It was a great talent, and using it may well have made her feel that she had some control in a life that was already showing signs of falling apart. At the very end of 1953, Monroe disappeared shortly before she was due to start filming *Pink Tights*, in which she was to play opposite Frank Sinatra. DiMaggio had whisked her away for a secret wedding.

Above and opposite: More studio portraits of Monroe from 1953. Despite her high intake of pills, Monroe's facial beauty was probably more at risk from make-up and studio lights.

A BAD SCENE

The marriage took place; the film was never made, placing Monroe technically in breach of her contract dated April 11, 1951. She was too important a player on the Twentieth Century-Fox scene to be brushed aside, though, on this occasion, she was disciplined. What should have caused the studio more concern was her drug problem, which was rapidly becoming more and more chronic.

Pill-popping was a major occupation in most branches of the entertainment industry in the 1950s. There were pills to see you through the day, to see you through the night, to keep you slim, to keep you happy, to keep you awake at work. Monroe took them all. Studio bosses knew she was addicted, but probably had no idea of the wide variety of drugs that she was taking. Directors and producers seemed unable or unwilling to link Monroe's often weird performance on set with any drug related cause.

She forgot her lines. She picked up the telephone before it rang. She drank from cups before she had poured coffee into them. She went through the studio make-up and hairdressing routine, and then decided she needed to shower. In her private life, she phoned friends at three in the morning, desperate or depressed or both. On the set of *How to Marry a Millionaire*, Nunally Johnson, Monroe's producer, was concerned. On location for *River of No Return*, a film Monroe made in 1954, director Otto Preminger was furious. It did not bode well for the long-term future.

Left: A studio shot of Monroe in the role of Rose Loomis for *Niagara*, May 21, 1952. The board identifies the costume designer as Dorothy Jeakins.
Right: Monroe poses by the mighty falls.

THE CAREER

As far as the critics and the public were concerned, however, Monroe could do little wrong. The critics had acclaimed her acting in *Niagara*, and had warmed to her vulnerable appeal as the short-sighted Pola Debevoise in *How to Marry a Millionaire*. Fans queued round the block to see all her movies. At a time when the movie business was first beginning to feel the pinch from television, Monroe was cinema's biggest attraction. Publicly, her work was admired by many of Hollywood's top directors. Henry Hathaway, director of *Niagara*, had found her both ambitious and talented. "She may not have had an education," he said, "but she was just naturally bright." Huston had praised her, and, for all her sudden lapses on set when she worked for him, Jean Negulesco adored her and labelled her a "star".

All her life, Monroe had longed to be a movie star. When stardom came, she couldn't believe it. "There was my name up in lights, I said 'God, somebody's made a mistake'. But there it was, in lights. And I sat there and said, 'Remember, you're not a star'. Yet there it was, up in lights."

NO BUSINESS LIKE SHOW BUSINESS

After the *Pink Tights* debacle, Monroe returned to studio favor, playing hat-check girl and *femme fatale* Vicky Hoffman in Fox's tribute to the songs of Irving Berlin – *There's No Business Like Show Business*. Her performance was rated poor by critics and audience alike. Monroe accepted the part only after Fox had promised her the female lead in *The Seven Year Itch*, a Broadway smash-hit play scheduled for filming in 1955.

There's No Business Like Show Business was filmed during one of Monroe's worst periods of drug abuse and at a time when she feared she might be going mad. Grace McKee, Monroe's substitute mother and guardian during her childhood, had recently committed suicide by taking an overdose of barbiturates in an asylum. It didn't help that when DiMaggio visited the set where Monroe was working at Fox, he took voluble exception to her being photographed in what he regarded as titillating costumes.

RIVER OF NO RETURN

Monroe did not welcome having to make the trip to the little town of Jasper, Alberta to shoot the location scenes for *River of No Return*. In the film she played the part of Kay Weston, a saloon bar singer in gold rush times. Her co-star was Robert Mitchum, who had worked alongside Monroe's first husband Jim Dougherty on a factory assembly line early in the Second World War. Mitchum and Monroe had a brief fling, rumors of which brought an angry Joe DiMaggio hot-footing up to the Canadian Rockies.

He was jealous, and he was violent.

It's hard to believe that Monroe and DiMaggio truly loved one another, easier to assume that each of them regarded the other as a trophy. Monroe wanted marriage as a prelude to having children; DiMaggio hoped marriage would tie her to him. After months of indecision, they finally took the plunge on January 14, 1954. Both were to be bitterly disappointed in the months that followed.

Opposite: A fine pair of chests... Robert Mitchum as Matt Calder, and Monroe as Kay Weston in a scene from *River of No Return*.

Above: Passion in front of the camera. It also took place off screen during location shooting for the film.

KOREA AND JAPAN

The official honeymoon was held in Tokyo, where DiMaggio had ended his professional baseball career two years earlier. For ten days vast crowds screamed their appreciation of the newlyweds, before Monroe went off on a three-day USO tour of American military stations in Korea. The war had been over for six months, but thousands of lonely, cold, frustrated soldiers were still safeguarding the uneasy peace.

In near freezing temperatures, Monroe donned her revealing costumes and belted out a selection of songs from her films and evergreen hits – including a censored version of *Do It Again*. The GIs and Marines loved every moment. Back in Tokyo, DiMaggio read the reports, watched the newsreels and was filled with jealousy yet again. When Monroe returned to Tokyo, she suffered a bout of pneumonia and a cracked thumb. Korean cold almost certainly caused the former. Italian rage may have been responsible for the latter.

NINE MONTH WONDER

It was not a happy marriage. Over the eight years left of her life, Monroe let out a steady trickle of truths and half-truths of what passed between her and DiMaggio in those miserable months. There were times when she ran from him, nights when neighbors heard blazing rows between the two of them, days when husband and wife never exchanged a word. DiMaggio's physical health suffered; Monroe's mental state came near to collapse.

DiMaggio was a traditionalist. He resented Monroe's career as much as he resented her ability to arouse other men and her penchant for flirting with them. To the Press, Monroe paid lip-service to the idea of being the little-woman-at-home, content to iron her man's shirts and cook his meals. In reality, she had not the slightest interest in pandering to DiMaggio's obsessive demands for order and tidiness. The sex was great, all else was dreadful.

DIVORCE

The end came mercifully quickly. Almost
immediately after she finished filming
There's No Business Like Show Business,
Monroe went to New York City to
shoot location scenes for *The Seven Year
Itch*. DiMaggio followed, arriving in time
to join the crowd watching his wife
being filmed on a Manhattan street for
the most famous scene in the film,
where Monroe stands over a grating as
her skirt billows up. He hated it and
hurried away. That night, there was
another row and, according to Monroe,
more violence.

A fortnight later, back in Hollywood,
Monroe called Billy Wilder – director of
The Seven Year Itch – to say she wouldn't
be reporting for work. She and Joe had
decided to put an end to their joint
miseries. Just 274 days after the
wedding, Monroe filed for divorce on
the grounds of mental cruelty. The
wonder was that the marriage had
lasted so long.

94 *Marilyn*

Horizontal once more... Monroe, in red brocade evening gown, uses her white fur stole as a pillow to pose for photographer Gene Lester in 1955. Lester worked for the *Saturday Evening Post, Silver Screen* and various Hollywood magazines in the 1950s.

THE NIGHT RAID

The divorce was granted on October 27, 1954. It has been said that Monroe opted to spend the night before the court hearing with DiMaggio, in Frank Sinatra's apartment. It was the end of the marriage, but not the end of the affair. Twentieth Century-Fox were worried that their most valuable investment was at risk. Hollywood divorces were often surrounded by or followed by scandal. They had Monroe watched. DiMaggio, now the jealous ex-husband, was hoping for an unlikely reconciliation. He hired a private detective to keep an eye on Monroe, presumably to check out the candidates for Monroe's next husband, for he suspected that she would not remain single for long. Nine days after the divorce, DiMaggio and Sinatra led a late-night raiding party on Monroe's apartment, hoping to catch her with a lover. Unfortunately, they chose the wrong apartment, and fled in disarray.

Right: Director Billy Wilder and
Monroe rehearse the studio
version of the famous grating scene
from *The Seven Year Itch*.
Left: Billy Wilder and Monroe
during rehearsals for *The Seven
Year Itch*.

THE
SEVEN
YEAR ITCH

Shooting both location and studio
scenes for *The Seven Year Itch* took place
between September 1 and 4 November
4, 1954 – the period leading up to and
including the Monroe–DiMaggio divorce.
In the film, Monroe played the part of
"The Girl", a model living in an
apartment above that of a man going
through what is now seen as a male
midlife crisis.

It was the first of two films that
Monroe made with Billy Wilder, a
director who deeply admired her work.
He described her as "an absolute genius
as a comedic actress, with an
extraordinary sense for comedic
dialogue. It was a God-given gift." The
film was a critical success and a box
office hit for Monroe, though it ran into
trouble from the censors at the Hays
Office. They took exception to the shot
of Monroe standing over the subway
grating, which had to be more modestly
recreated in the studio. Perhaps
DiMaggio felt his rage that night in
Manhattan had been justified.

MARILYN MONROE—20th Century-Fox Player
Made in U.S.A.

Left and right: Two studio publicity shots of Monroe taken at the time she was filming *The Seven Year Itch*. Fox never tired of getting Monroe in front of the camera for the most routine of sessions.

ART IMITATING LIFE

The Seven Year Itch started life as a stage play by George Axelrod, who made sure that some of his original dialogue survived in the movie. In one scene, Monroe – the smart blonde playing the dumb blonde – delivers an impassioned speech describing the greater attraction of the pensive male over the athletic male.

"You think every girl's a dope? You think a girl goes to a party and there's this one guy, a great big hunk in a fancy striped vest strutting around like a tiger, giving you that 'I'm so handsome you can't resist me look?' And from this she's supposed to fall flat on her face? Well, she doesn't fall flat on her face. But there's another guy in the room... Maybe he's kind of nervous and shy... First you look past him, but then you sort of sense he's gentle and kind... and he'll be tender with you... That's what's really exciting..."

In real life, Monroe was about to make the move from DiMaggio to Miller.

FLIGHT FROM LA

The traditional end-of-filming party for *The Seven Year Itch* took place in December 1954 at Romanoff's, the restaurant run by the man Life magazine had dubbed America's "Most Wonderful Liar" – Harry Gerguson, alias Prince Michael Romanoff. It was an appropriate setting for the insincerity that flowed that night as Hollywood turned out in force to honour Monroe. All the big names were there: Sam Goldwyn, Jack Warner, Darryl Zanuck, Bogart and Bacall, Susan Hayward, James Stewart, William Holden, Gary Cooper, and the man who had long been Monroe's dream father – Clark Gable.

Not for the first or the last time in her life, Monroe believed that at last she had made it. She was accepted. She was a star. She was somebody. It was a time to stay put, luxuriate in her new status, consolidate her position, enjoy the fruits of her success. What Monroe did, however, was run away.

Left: Monroe as Kay Weston, the saloon bar chanteuse in *River of No Return*.
Right: Monroe as pole-dancer. She once accidentally poked her finger in the eye of a male dancer during a shoot, but immediately gave him an impromptu "make-it-better" kiss.

"The body is meant to be seen, not all covered up."

"My illusions didn't have anything
to do with being a fine actress.
I knew how third rate I was.
I could actually feel my lack
of talent, as if it were cheap clothes
I was wearing inside. But, my God,
how I wanted to learn,
to change, to improve!"

Monroe reads *To the Actor* by Michael Chekhov,
as she relaxes in a New York restaurant, March
1955. He was her acting coach at the time.

Left and right: "… she likes the theater, but never comes late…" (Lorenz Hart). Monroe applies the finishing touches to her appearance before setting off from her New York hotel to see the Broadway production of the Tennessee Williams play *Cat on a Hot Tin Roof*, on March 24, 1955.

4

PART QUEEN, PART WAIF

Monroe's attempt to escape the clutches of Hollywood in the mid-1950s was fuelled by both personal and professional longings. Though the everlasting child in her still loved the glitz and glamor of Tinseltown, Monroe had ambitions to be seen as a serious actor, accompanied by a mounting desire to form her own production company, free from the shackles of Zanuck and Twentieth Century-Fox. Coupled with this, she wanted to move to the other side of the continent, to distance herself from DiMaggio and his spies, and from the crop of painful memories that her life in California had so plentifully supplied since childhood.

And so she flew to New York City (*right*), to start a new business, to enrol at the Actors Studio, and coincidentally to renew her acquaintance with Arthur Miller. He'd first met her at a Hollywood party some years earlier, when Evelyn Keyes had pointed her out, surrounded by rivals and exploiters. "Look at her," she had said. "They'll eat her alive." Miller was immediately smitten.

THE PINK ELEPHANT

Even in sophisticated Manhattan, it was impossible for Monroe to escape demands that she lend the most famous body in the world for publicity purposes. This time, however, the publicity was wanted for a good cause. On March 31, 1955, introduced by "ringmaster" Milton Berle, Monroe entered Madison Square Garden on top of a pink elephant, to raise money for a charity seeking to combat arthritis. The circus had come to town.

As was the case with many events in Monroe's career, echoes of that pink elephant day came down to her later in life. Milton Berle had a small part in Monroe's 1960 film *Let's Make Love*, and "riding the pink elephant" became the code name that Monroe used for sleeping with President Kennedy.

Doubtful faces study the costume Monroe wore when she entered Madison Square Garden on a pink elephant to raise money for charity, New York City, March 1955. In the end, the costume was approved.

THE STUDENT

Monroe's flight to New York brought her new friends, a new environment, and the opportunity to fulfil a long-held ambition – to take herself seriously as an actress. She spent her weekends in Connecticut with the photographer Milton Greene and his family, and her weeks in the city, sightseeing and planning the next step in her career. In the spring of 1955, she enrolled at the Actors Studio. At the time, Lee Strasberg's acting school was regarded as the most prestigious in the world and the Stanislavsky Method was highly acclaimed by many of the biggest names in the business.

Strasberg interviewed Monroe. He was intrigued by her account of her life, which may well have been highly colored, and agreed to take her on as a private pupil for three months.

Part teacher, part shrink, and part guru, he pounced on what he saw as inner conflict in Monroe: "...what she looked like was not what she really was, and what was going on inside her was not what was going on outside, and that always means there may be something to work with."

Opposite: Despite the presence of the photographer, Monroe rides the New York subway apparently unobserveded by her fellow passengers, March 24, 1955.

Above: At the end of the ride, Monroe is recognized on Grand Central Station.

After three months, Strasberg allowed Monroe to join classes with other students. These were not youngsters starting out on their careers, but experienced actors who could recognize talent, or lack of it, and they were impressed by both Monroe's dedication and her ability, although at first she was too scared to even open her mouth. Among them was Kim Stanley, who was the original Cherie in *Bus Stop* when it opened as a Broadway play – the part Monroe was to play in the 1956 film. Stanley was among those who applauded Monroe's readings from Shakespeare, Chekhov, and O'Neill: "We were taught never to clap at the Actors Studio. It was like we were in church. It was the first time I'd ever heard applause there."

Monroe's fragile self-image gained strength from her spell at the Studio. "For the first time," she said, "I felt accepted not as a freak but as myself." Her admiration for Strasberg developed into a reverence. Arthur Miller, who was keeping a close eye on Monroe at the time, noted what was happening, but reckoned that Monroe needed to develop some kind of faith "after years in the cynical Hollywood jungle".

Opposite: Monroe turns to director Joshua Logan for advice while shooting location scenes in Arizona for the Twentieth Century-Fox movie *Bus Stop*.
Left: In the same costume, Monroe poses for a publicity shot.

BUS STOP

Monroe left New York and Connecticut in February 1956 to return to Twentieth Century-Fox. She was cast as hillbilly café singer Cheryl in Joshua Logan's *Bus Stop,* a performance that won her the Golden Globe Award for Best Motion Picture Actress in a Comedy or Musical. Logan, himself a graduate of the Stanislavsky school, joined Monroe's rapidly growing number of professional admirers: "Marilyn is as near a genius as any actress... She is an artist beyond artistry. She is the most completely realized and authentic film actress since Garbo."

Monroe unceremoniously discarded her old acting coach, Natasha Lytess,

replacing her with Lee Strasberg's wife, Paula. It was an unkind action, but it paid dividends. Paula Strasberg was always on hand in the studio, protecting Monroe's still flimsy ego, keeping the Press at bay, and dispensing Monroe's pills.

What neither her coach, her director or her studio knew, was that Monroe was conducting a clandestine series of telephone conversations with Arthur Miller, who was in Nevada, arranging his divorce. A new period in her life was about to begin.

THE PRINCESS AND THE PLAYWRIGHT

In the mid-1950s Arthur Miller was arguably the most famous and most successful playwright in the Western world. He had already written four of his greatest plays (*All My Sons, Death of a Salesman, The Crucible* and *A View from the Bridge*) and had honorably withstood spiteful investigation by McCarthy and the House Un-American Activities Committee.

He had known Monroe on and off since 1951 and had become irresistibly attracted to her. He had been married for over fifteen years and had spent the last two or three years wrestling with his conscience, seeing a future with her as a possible "doom beyond all knowing". But his sexual longing for her was too powerful to be denied.

Monroe was deeply attracted to the playwright. She admired Miller for his intellect, and saw in him the warmth and sympathy that she craved all her life. It's simplistic to say that he was a father figure to her. Every man Monroe had personal or professional relations with filled that role – either as a good or bad father.

Opposite: Joy before marriage… Arthur Miller and Monroe on the Connecticut farm that Miller shared with Milton Greene, June 27, 1956. Two days later, they were married.
Above: Love before marriage... For Miller, it was the best of times.

"OH, PAPA, I CAN'T DO IT..."

The courtship of Monroe and Miller was conducted under difficult circumstances. There was the obvious complication of Miller's existing marriage, and the less obvious one of DiMaggio's prowling hopes of reconciliation with Monroe. As ever, there were other men, and Monroe had a brief affair with Marlon Brando. Allegedly, there was also another abortion. Strangest of all, the shipping magnate Aristotle Onassis had a plan to arrange a marriage between Monroe and Prince Rainier of Monaco, largely for business reasons. Monroe did not reject the idea out of hand, but was mightily relieved when the role went to Grace Kelly.

For Miller and Monroe, the times when they were together – in Monroe's apartment, in diners, on the sidewalks of New York – were fine. Separation was intolerable for both. When Monroe returned to Hollywood to make *Bus Stop,* there were long and painful phone calls. Monroe was again pulverized by self-doubt. "Oh, Papa," she sobbed down the line to Miller, "I can't do it... I can't fight them alone, I want to live with you in the country and be a good wife..." Miller's Reno divorce came through.

Honeymooners abroad.
Opposite and left: Monroe and Miller pose for the camera outside their rented home in Englefield Green, Surrey, July 17, 1956. Both appreciated the peace of the English countryside, and what Miller regarded as the old world ways of the English.

What she did best... The eyes heavy with longing, the head held high, the lips parted in promise, the doors of the dress opening to the cleavage... The camera pays homage to Monroe at the height of her bodily power in the mid-1950s.

AN ENGLISH HONEYMOON

For the second time in her life, Monroe interrupted a judge's dinner with a call that His Honor come to officiate at her wedding. Judge Seymour Robinowitz performed a simple civil ceremony in the heat of a New York summer, followed two days later by a Jewish wedding at the home of Miller's agent. Monroe promised that any children of the marriage would be raised in the Jewish faith. Bride, groom, and friends then shared an outdoor wedding breakfast of lobster, turkey, and champagne.

The honeymoon was spent in England. After another menacing encounter with McCarthy's mob, Miller's passport was returned in time to fly to London, where work awaited both newlyweds. Miller had a new production of *A View from the Bridge* to oversee, and Monroe had another film to make. After a twelve hour flight, they were hauled to the biggest press conference in English history. They rented a house from the publisher of the *Financial Times* in the heart of the Surrey countryside, and were awakened on the first morning by a choir of 100 men and boys singing an *aubade* below their bedroom window.

126 *Marilyn*

Two shots of Monroe as she hosts a party for members of the Press at her apartment in Los Angeles, March 1956. She was just approaching her thirtieth birthday.

GLAMOR GIRL

Though she was still able to travel *incognito* in dark glasses and unfashionable clothes – provided she kept the wiggle in check – Monroe was now far and away the most famous woman in the world. Only eight years had passed since her first film appearance, uncredited, in *Scudda Hoy!* Now she was a world star, which meant she was also common property, a cardboard cut-out, a parody of herself. She was the ultimate sex symbol, presented as the siren all men desired.

There were those in Hollywood who prized her as a commodity but despised her as a human being, who longed to banish her from the movie business but would have done anything to keep her there, for she was the swan that laid the golden eggs. Everywhere she looked there were people who wanted her, but did little to show that they liked her. And, as for love, Monroe continued to want it and test it to destruction.

PICTURE POST

POLAND'S REVOLT
—Exclusive pictures

PIRIE'S GLORIOUS "FAILURE"

DORS in HOLLYWOOD

BRITAIN'S ATOMIC COALMINE

TYSON and EVANS

BEDTIME WITH MARILYN
See inside

THE PRINCE AND THE SHOWGIRL

Monroe's effect on all things English was startling. Wherever she went, whatever she did, whatever she said became front page news. When she visited a large new Marks and Spencer store in the West End of London, the shop was emptied of all other customers. When she fell ill, she was attended by the Queen's obstetrician. Her waxwork was unveiled at Madame Tussaud's. Despite her protestation that she was "just Mrs Miller tonight", her scarlet, cling-tight, mermaid dress stole much of Miller's thunder at the opening night of his play.

She captured the hearts of one and all, including that of Laurence Olivier, who initially had considerable doubts about her acting abilities, but came to see her as "an extremely skilled actress". It was an odd pairing. When he heard of Olivier's plans to make *The Prince and the Showgirl* with Monroe, Noel Coward thought the experience might conceivably drive the stage knight "round the bend". Paula Strasberg was also on hand, to protect Monroe, to irritate Olivier, and to provide advice on acting that Miller regarded as gobbledygook.

Opposite: Surrounded by the Press,
Monroe takes tea at the Savoy Hotel,
London, July 17, 1956. Olivier is on her right.
Above: Olivier and Monroe exchange a
few words at the press conference.

Monroe, as the chorus girl Elsie Marina,
prepares for the first scene to be shot for
The Prince and the Showgirl, August 7, 1956.
Jack Cardiff, Director of Photography, saw
"the differences between Larry and Marilyn
grow as they became more tense and tired."

ELSIE MARINA

The Prince and the Showgirl was based on
Terence Rattigan's stage play *The
Sleeping Prince*. The film was made by
Warner Brothers and Monroe's own
production company, and was filmed in
London. Monroe played Elsie Marina, an
Edwardian chorus girl who captures the
heart of the Prince Regent of Carpathia.
Some critics found the film charming,
most panned it. For both Olivier and
Monroe, it was an unpleasant
experience. She thought he was a bully.
He thought she was stupid, lazy, and
unprofessional. Until banished from the
set by Olivier, Paula Strasberg proved
Monroe's main support, telling Monroe
she was "the greatest human being of all
time." Olivier was astonished.

It was a deeply upsetting time for
Monroe. Cracks began to appear in her
relationships with Milton Greene, her
business associate, and with Miller. Her
reliance on pills increased and she
started drinking early in the morning.
She suffered waves of suicidal despair. In
November 1956, an exhausted and
unhappy Monroe returned to the
United States.

Left: Monroe and Miller arrive at the Empire, Leicester Square for the Royal Command Film Premiere of *The Prince and the Showgirl*, October 1956.
Opposite: At London's Comedy Theatre for the opening night of *A View from the Bridge*.

PICTURE
POST
MONDAY 22 OCTOBER 1956
TAMING THE MAU MAU–
Dramatic Picture Exclusive
THE MOTOR SHOW–
The new ideas
Marilyn makes
headlines again
See inside
4D
HULTON'S
NATIONAL
WEEKLY

BANDAGING HER WOUNDS

Back home, Monroe and Miller did what they could to mend their marriage. Monroe took a two year break from filming. Miller approved. He saw filming as "a kind of siege" for Monroe, "during which she needed eyes in the back of her head". There were the on-set rows with studio officials, the demands of publicity departments and the Press, the fads and fancies of her fellow actors, the strain and drain of having to be beautiful and sexy at all times. What Miller called "the toll of her stardom" acted as an addictive and destructive drug every bit as much as the barbiturates and amphetamines she swallowed by the fistful. Monroe talked of wanting to go back to school, to study, to learn, to read novels, to get involved in politics. "I'd love to learn how things got to be how they are," she told Miller.

Miller and Monroe moved out of Manhattan and rented a house on the eastern tip of Long Island. Miller struggled to write a new play. Monroe learned how to cook and make her own noodles. They walked on the beach and chatted with local fishermen. Marilyn wrote poetry and learned to swim. For a couple of blissful months, Monroe was pregnant. But the pregnancy was diagnosed as tubal and Monroe had to return to New York to have it terminated. Tragically, the termination resulted in a breach in what had previously been a good relationship between Monroe and her mother-in-law.

So many pictures were taken of Monroe, year after year, that some photographers became desperate in their attempts to find a new angle on glamour. In this 1957 studio session, Monroe was asked to romp with a cuddly toy. It got worse later.

Long Island held no magic properties. One night, not long after the pregnancy was terminated, Miller discovered Monroe slumped in an armchair, deep in a drug-induced coma. He summoned an emergency medical team who saved her life. It was time to leave.

Back in New York things began to fall apart once more. Monroe blamed her own drug-taking for the failure of her pregnancy, called for vodka first thing in the morning, spent her days in idle misery. Once more, they tried moving to a new location – this time to a 300-acre farm in Connecticut. Once more, the cameras followed them. Once more, Monroe put on make-up, costume, and smile, and posed for them. Once more, the resulting pictures were gobbled up by hungry magazines.

Monroe developed a great interest in wildlife. On Long Island, she had scurried up and down the beach, throwing the dying fish that had been rejected by the fishermen back into the sea. In New York, on a daily basis, she bought pigeons that had been trapped by young boys and released them into the wild. In Roxbury, she adopted stray dog.

A
LAST
GIFT

The problems that Miller and Monroe faced in their marriage sprang from the incompatibility of two artists. Miller felt the creative part of his life was slipping away while so much of his time was taken up in looking after Monroe. She, in turn, felt that his writing ate into time that should have been spent looking after her. Sometimes she could recognise that she was being unreasonable in her demands, but the misery and the emotional sickness within her too often pushed all reason to the side.

The irony was that Miller was working on a present for her. He had written a short story called *The Misfits*, about a bunch of modern day cowboys. While Monroe was in hospital, Sam Shaw, one of the many Monroe photographers, told Miller that the story would make a great movie, 'and that's a woman's part she could kick into the stands'. Miller immediately began work on turning the story into a screenplay, which he saw as a gift for the woman he still loved.

CHAPTER FIVE

THE MOST FRAGILE AND LOVEABLE LEGEND OF ALL

When it came, the final plunge into darkness was swift and unstoppable. Monroe spun dizzily into a nightmare world, populated by Mafia mobsters, powerful politicians, FBI agents, the greatest names in showbiz, rogues and charlatans, false gurus and false friends. She adored and trusted the wrong people, and in the end it was impossible to save her. The last scene of the tragedy was brief, played out in a shoddy bedroom littered with pill capsules and booze bottles, and with all the rest of the squalor that abject loneliness can bring. And then the rumors began — of conspiracy, murder, and betrayal; of falsified records; of mysterious helicopters clattering through the night; of a macabre visit to the dying Monroe by one of the Kennedys.

Before that, there were three last films — *Some Like It Hot*, *The Misfits* (*right*), and *Let's Make Love* (*above*) — one more divorce, the hopes of yet another marriage, a handful of last flings, and hundreds more studio portraits.

Above: Sugar Kane sings one of the numbers from *Some Like It Hot.*
Opposite: Monroe, with Jack Lemmon (*center*) and Tony Curtis filming *Some Like It Hot.*

"I don't mind living in a man's world
as long as I can be a woman in it.."

SOME LIKE IT HOT

Monroe made thirty films, though her last – *Something's Got to Give* – was never completed. The best of the bunch, in terms of longevity and popular appeal, was Billy Wilder's *Some Like It Hot,* made for United Artists in 1959. For those making it, the film was a nightmare. Monroe was constantly hours late for work. She verbally abused the crew. She threw tantrums about her appearance, her co-stars, and the way Wilder framed his shots. "When Marilyn Monroe comes into a room," she sneered, "nobody's going to be looking

at Tony Curtis playing Joan Crawford. They're going to be looking at Marilyn Monroe."

Not surprisingly, Monroe's unpredictability, lack of co-operation and outright rudeness made Wilder ill. And yet, he knew before the film was finished that she had done a wonderful job, that her indefinable magic had produced a performance that no other actor could give. In the years that followed, long after Monroe's death, he'd start working on projects and think: "It's not going to work. It needs Marilyn Monroe. Nobody

else is in that orbit; everyone else is earthbound by comparison."

Filming took five months, during which time Monroe was again pregnant. She considered pulling out of *Some Like It Hot.* Miller advised against it, and Monroe wondered if he was losing his enthusiasm for her to have a baby – he already had children. Once filming was finished, Monroe flew back to New York. Just before Christmas 1959, she lost the baby. The marriage headed for the rocks.

Monroe as Amanda Dell in George Cukor's
Let's Make Love. In the film Monroe yet
again played a showgirl.

LET'S MAKE LOVE, AND LET'S MAKE WHOOPEE

Miller pressed on with the screenplay he was writing as a present for Monroe, while Monroe continued to go through the motions of being a star. In September 1959, the Soviet leader Nikita Khrushchev came to Hollywood. Monroe took her customary four or five hours in make-up and arrived at the lunch in Khrushchev's honor. He stopped to speak to her, perhaps regarding her as the most impressive product the United States had to offer.

Monroe was now in her mid-thirties. Her marriage to Miller was failing. It was time to deal it a death blow. She started an affair. Following the success of *Some Like It Hot*, Twentieth Century-Fox cast Monroe opposite the French singer and actor Yves Montand in a light comedy musical, called *Let's Make Love*. They did. During filming, they lived in neighboring bungalows at the Beverly Hills Hotel, with their respective unsuspecting spouses. Then Miller flew east to work, and Montand's wife – Simone Signoret – had to return to Paris. All went well in bed, but Monroe fell in love with Montand. It was not reciprocated.

THE MISFITS

As he neared the end of the first draft of *The Misfits*, Miller had thought of John Huston as the film's director. He remembered Huston's rough kindness to Monroe on the set of *The Asphalt Jungle* some ten years earlier, and he foresaw the need for kindness, tolerance, and patience in abundance right now. The coffin that contained the remains of the Miller–Monroe marriage was about to be lowered into the ground.

The cast that assembled in Reno when shooting began in August 1960 was impressive. Monroe's co-stars included her beloved Clark Gable, Montgomery Clift, Eli Wallach, and Thelma Ritter. But there were problems. Gable's health was declining and he never really understood the script. Clift was moody and depressed. Huston spent many nights drinking and gambling. There was friction between Miller and Huston, and, as ever, Paula Strasberg was there to interfere and complicate matters. When a British reporter visited the set of *The Misfits*, he felt it was "like standing in a minefield among all those manic-depressive people".

But the big problem was Monroe. The loss of her baby had destroyed what little hope and inner strength she had. She talked of suicide, though not to Miller or anyone who might have been able to do something to help her. When she reported for work – often hours late – she was chock-full of drugs or alcohol. Early on, Huston had to send her away for a detox. The wonder was that the film was made.

Four studies by photographer Ernst Haas, taken on location with *The Misfits* in 1960. **Left to right:** Gable and Monroe; Wallach and Monroe; Monroe on set; Huston and Monroe on the dry Nevada lake bed.

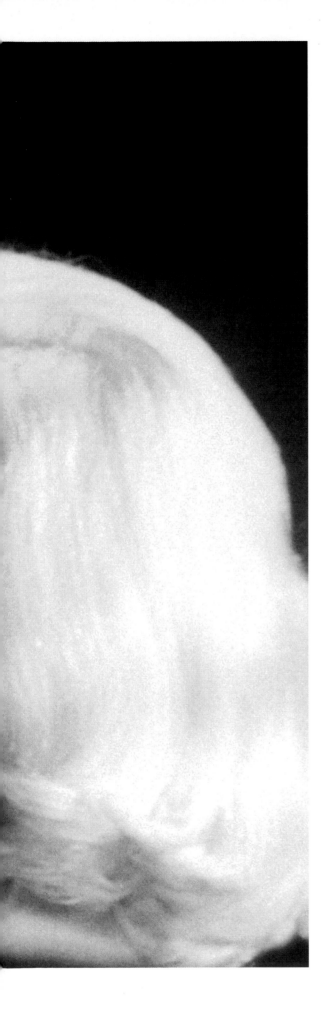

Yves Montand and Monroe. Before he began filming *Let's Make Love*, Montand had never seen a Monroe film. At first, Montand found working with her irritating and tiresome, and he accused her of being a "capricious little girl".

THE LIGHT STILL BURNS

Despite all the misery, drugs, booze, and despair, Monroe still had the power to seduce any man she set her sights on, and to impress her professional colleagues. Clift adored her. "I would rather work with her than any other actress," he said. Huston spoke of Monroe as having "no techniques – it was all truth".

Some of the praise lavished on her may be sentimental, uttered after her death, in the soft light of tragedy, but not in the case of Gable, who predeceased

her, dying of a heart attack three days after filming finished. "Marilyn is a kind of ultimate," he said. "She is uniquely feminine. Everything she does is different, strange and exciting, from the way she talks to the way she used that magnificent torso. She makes a man proud to be a man." They are hardly the words that a father should use when speaking of a daughter, but maybe Monroe's life would have been happier if her real father could have told her that she made him proud.

Two scenes from *Let's Make Love*.
Opposite: Monroe with Frankie Vaughan.
In the film, Vaughan played Mr Nice Guy, who
doesn't get the girl – as in art, so in life...
Above: Monroe displaying one of most
famous expressions – the open-mouth
amazement.

Fighting her way through crowds.
Opposite: Monroe takes on the Press after announcing her separation from Arthur Miller, New York City, November 1960.
Left: Monroe leaves hospital after gall-bladder surgery, July 11, 1961.

THE PACK MOVES CLOSER

As soon as shooting finished on *The Misfits*, Monroe and Miller flew back to New York... on separate flights. There was still time for a few more tragic scenes in Monroe's life. She was deeply upset by news of Gable's death, assuming guilt where none existed. She and Miller discussed arrangements for what had become the inevitable divorce, working out how best to announce the sad news to the voracious Press and the public hordes. They decided to go to Mexico, and on January 20, 1961, the four-and-a-half year marriage was ended by a judge in Ciudad Juarez. It had been the longest and perhaps the best marriage of her life.

Ironically, it was another of her ex-husbands who now rallied to her support. Joe DiMaggio's strange and erratic love for Monroe still burned. He brought her flowers. He helped her to hospital when she fell ill with internal pains which some unkindly and inaccurately diagnosed as purely psychological in origin. His love was, yet again, too little, too late.

BETWEEN TWO KENNEDYS

There are things we know about relations between both Jack and Robert Kennedy and Monroe, and things we know we don't know. Almost certainly, there are things we don't know we don't know. Monroe first met Jack Kennedy in the early 1950s, and may have had a brief affair with him during her marriage to DiMaggio, but the key period is the last few months of Monroe's tortured life.

Tales abound of meetings between Jack and Monroe, of intimate dinners, of visits to beach houses in Santa Monica, and of assignations in hotel suites. Some rumors go further, suggesting that Jack passed Monroe on to Robert Kennedy, and that Monroe was having an affair with Frank Sinatra while flitting from one Kennedy to another. What seems certain is that Monroe genuinely admired Jack Kennedy and believed he was a great man. And whenever Monroe admired a man for his mind, she was prepared to offer herself in homage.

Opposite: Perhaps the most poignant moment in her life... Monroe sings "Happy Birthday to You" to President Kennedy at the Democrat Rally, Madison Square Garden, May 19, 1962.
Above: After the Rally... (*from left to right*) Bobby Kennedy, Monroe, and the President.

A sheet of contact prints from the last interview and photo session given by Monroe. The pictures were taken at her home on Fifth Helena Drive, Brentwood, California by photographer Allan Grant just three weeks before her death.

Opposite: The front pages of the *New York Mirror* and the *Daily Post* for August 6, 1962, the day after Monroe's death
Above: The room in which Monroe died.

The funeral of Marilyn Monroe at
Westwood Memorial Park, Hollywood,
August 13, 1962.
Opposite: Members of the funeral party
include Joe DiMaggio (*third from left*) and
Bernice Miracle, Monroe's half sister (*fourth
from right*)
Right: A tearful DiMaggio at the funeral.

When it came, the end was ugly.
Monroe was fired from Fox's musical
Something's Got To Give in the spring of
1962. Daily visits to her psychiatrist
didn't prevent her from cramming yet
more prescription pills into her mouth,
feigning illness, and plunging into a
darkness where depression and
desperation fought for possession of her.
She moved to a new house, shopped
for furnishings, bought plants for the
garden. It made no difference.

On the night of August 3, 1962,
Monroe slept badly. When her
psychiatrist, Ralph Gleeson, visited her
the following afternoon he was glad she
had no sleeping pills, there was a hint of
suicidal thoughts. Some eleven hours
later, at three in the morning of August
5, he received a phone call from
Monroe's housekeeper and hurried over.
He found Monroe face down on her
bed, with the phone clutched in her
hand. By the side of the bed was an
empty bottle of Nembutal, a powerful
sleeping pill. Monroe was dead.

Left: A porcelain figure of Monroe in the famous subway ventilator grill scene from *The Seven Year Itch*. Nearly fifty years after her death, memorabilia's of Monroe's life still make record sales around the world.
Right: Red roses on Monroe's crypt.

LAST RITES

Dr. Greeson phoned the police, who arrived too late to seal the room from the intrusions of a couple of lucky reporters. Monroe's body was removed to the Hall of Justice, where a none-too-thorough *post mortem* examination was performed. After rapid consultations, the official cause of death was fixed as suicide by means of an overdose of sleeping pills. Sinatra and the Kennedys distanced themselves from Monroe with all speed.

Monroe's few true friends did what they could for her. It fell to Whitey Snyder, Monroe's long-time make-up man, to restore her body from the ravages of the autopsy, and to prepare it for the coffin. Joe DiMaggio, the man whose nervous, jumpy love for Monroe had never died, supervised the funeral arrangements. He wanted to keep it a private affair, but it proved impossible to keep the hordes of photographers and reporters from Westwood Memorial Park. "Be sure," he said, "that none of those damn Kennedys come to the funeral." He had his way. For the next twenty years, three times a week, he left red roses by her simple headstone.

There were few relatives to mourn Monroe. Her mother and half-sister, Bernice Miracle, survived her, but she had no father – and no father-figure after the death of Gable – and no children. Lee Strasberg delivered a strange eulogy, in which he stressed Monroe's luminosity, wistfulness, radiance, and yearning "that set her apart and made everyone wish to be a part of it".

The most widely recognised face in the history of the world.

Left: The design for the US 29 cent postage stamp, issued in 1995.

Opposite: Andy Warhol's famous 1964 portrait, based on a 1952 publicity still.

THE MONROE MYSTERY

Conspiracy theorists have brought Jack Kennedy and Marilyn Monroe together in a bizarre life-after-death riddled with coincidence. Kennedy died some fifteen months after Monroe, in very different circumstances, but to those who do not accept the official versions of either's death, there are remarkable similarities. In both cases, there have been rumors of Mafia involvement, of FBI or CIA interference and possible complicity, of secret orders issued by J. Edgar Hoover, of bungled *post mortem* examinations, of missing documents, and of police incompetence.

There have even been outright accusations that Monroe was murdered. If she swallowed dozens of pills, why was there no water carafe or glass by her bedside? Who made the series of mysterious phone calls to Monroe that last night? And who did she call? Was Bobby Kennedy in Brentwood that night, and, if so, why? Did he in fact visit Monroe while she lay dying, realise what was happening and hurry to a helicopter to whisk him away? And who subsequently tampered with the records of the helicopter charter company? The questions will almost certainly never be answered, but there are no signs as yet of their going away.

In the end, what remains of Monroe's lonely, broken-hearted, crazy life is a handful of movies, some notorious photographic images, and the fading memories passed down by her ever-decreasing band of former colleagues. The world will never forget her, but will maybe one day wonder why it remembers the star who, in the words of the author Edward Wagenknecht "played the best game with the worst hand".

"To have survived, she would have had to be either more cynical or even further from reality than she was.

Instead, she was a poet on a street corner trying to recite to a crowd pulling at her clothes."

Arthur Miller

To my dear sister
love Norma Jeane

Marilyn was created in conjunction with Getty Images. Particular thanks go to Jonathan Hyams and Paul Chesne at the Michael Ochs Collection. The design was initiated by Paul Welti but created and executed by Ros Holder. Author Nick Yapp worked with picture researcher Ali Khoja. Mark Fletcher edited, Liz Ihre was project co-ordinator and Mary Osborne led the production.

Fall River Press
122 Fifth Avenue
New York, NY 10011

ISBN 978-1-4351-1501-9

Printed in Singapore
10 9 8 7 6 5 4 3 2 1

All images courtesy of **Getty Images** including the following which have additional attributions:

t top, m middle, b bottom

Agence France Presse: 118, 171; **Evan Agostini:** 1; **Columbia Pictures:** 30; **Frank Driggs:** 43, 117; **I.M. Garrett:** 48, 67 (l & m); **Ernst Haas:** 143, 150, 151, 152, 153 (all); **Darlene Hammond:** 68, 69, 72; **IPC/Picture Post:** 70, 129, 136; **John Kobal Foundation:** 28, 29, 41, 56, 66, 138-9, 147; **Gene Lester:** 85, 94-5; **Silver Screen Collection:** 7, 8-9, 13, 14, 15, 16, 17, 18-19, 20, 21, 22-3; **Time and Life Pictures:** 26, 38, 40, 52, 53, 62, 64, 65, 67 (r), 71, 73, 86, 87, 89, 93, 119, 120, 121, 140, 141, 154-5, 159, 160, 161, 162-3, 164, 168, 169, 170.